Case Notes

Case Notes

by

Judith Wozniak

First published 2024 by The Hedgehog Poetry Press,

5 Coppack House, Churchill Avenue, Clevedon. BS21 6QW

www.hedgehogpress.co.uk

ISBN: 978-1-916830-03-5

for Hannah and Mike

Contents

CHANGELING

She has barricaded herself upstairs with her baby.
I talk my way into a room backlit by a streetlamp.
Her words trip over each other. She found a sign,

a feather hidden under his cot. She was told
he was born with a caul. He should have been safe.
It's his smell. She's certain this baby is not hers.

He's lying so still, his face a mask, bone-white,
translucent eyelids traced with inky capillaries.
Then he stirs, holds up a chubby hand

fingers splay as he dreams, slowly curl back,
folding his thumb in a dimpled fist. He startles
as I lift him, hold his warm milky sleepiness.

Her gaze fixed on the open window, a shudder
of cold rattles the latch. Nets caught on a breeze
sail into the room. She sees an angel.

FIRST DO NO HARM

After Hippocrates

He staggers out across our path
drapes his arms around me.
Just a lad — at first we laugh
we think he is drunk.

A peony shaped stain spreads crimson
over my best navy dress, with silk ties.
We are on our way out to celebrate
making it through the first year.

He starts to claw the air,
his face pale as candle-wax.
I'm kneeling in his spilled blood,
splashed flecks stiffen my face.

I feel it seep, sticky between my thighs,
press my ear against his chest,
listen for a heart-beat.
People gather — we fend them off.

Don't worry we are all doctors.
We don't believe it ourselves,
long for the sound of a siren
the rotating pulse of blue light,

the safety of the hospital, the crash team
running, the clatter of drip stands.
Hours spent learning lists, practising procedures,
and all we can do — is to wait.

PEGGY AND GEORGE

Before I can put my bag down.
a cup of tea is pressed into my hands,
biscuits in a puddled saucer.

I've come back to check on George,
The tug and heave of his breath,
eased since yesterday. Peggy hovers

making her curious clicking noises
with her mouth. Her loose dentures
oscillate to their own rhythm.

She peers up, squeezes her face.
I'm not wearing the Rimmel lipstick
she gave me, she worries I'm too pale.

They have shrunk over time
to fit into their sheltered home,
squashed together with their trinkets.

She has hardly left the house for years.
Once to visit George in hospital
and for their golden wedding buffet

at the Red Lion. Stooped together
like brackets, Peggy fidgeting
with the clasp of her best necklace.

Guests of honour, the district nurse,
unrecognisable, loosened from her tight bun,
and me with my sunset orange lips.

SARAH BERNHARDT'S LEG

After Dr Pozzi at Home, John Singer Sargent

I first saw her emerge from the Odéon,
a froth of silk and feathers, unfazed
by the mizzle jewelling her hair, spun

sugar, glistening in a loop of gaslight
her skin moon-pale, a glimpse
of shapely ankle in a satin slipper.

She persuaded me to pose for my portrait
in blood red robes, the thick tassel
hanging from a cord belt amused her.

The fall should have destroyed her.
I could never again watch Tosca
leaping from the parapet.

Her letters implored me to intervene
*my beloved Doctor God -- I beg you
to cut off my leg. A little above the knee.*

She was wheeled to the operating theatre
in a white silk peignoir, veiled in rose
crepe de chine, whistling The Marseilles.

My courageous Lady of the Camellias,
they say it was her finest performance.

SECOND OPINION

By the time I arrive she's already in her nightclothes
feet steadied in oversized slippers with a fur-ruff.

The heating is set to tropical, my glasses steam up,
I settle on the sofa. This could take some time.

I struggle to extract clues, check red flags, hidden agendas,
examine vital signs. I try charming her, *you're like my mother,*

she is delighted. I'm getting weary now, one last try.
Is anything else worrying you? Tomorrow's the wedding

— her granddaughter's. She has been warned
not to let the family down. She disappears to her bedroom,

returns wearing a huge hat like the Quangle Wangle's.
It's feathered, beribboned, quivering. I peer underneath

wipe a trickle of tears from her chin. It needs a minor op.
With her informed consent I tease out two pheasant feathers,

a cluster of plastic cherries then use my sterile scissors to trim
the organza bow. She beams at her reflection. *It's amazing* I say.

A ROUTINE HOUSE CALL

I hear her reedy voice, the tap of a stick,
wait while she struggles to unbolt the door.
Not her usual doctor, I smile my way in
like a salesman. Her cardigan rides up

over a spine curved like an upturned hull,
a pink scalp peeps through a fuss of curls.
She eases herself slowly into her chair,
sinks into a puff of dust and talc.

I turn her hands over in mine. The fan
of bones collapse against each other.
Her skin crinkles like the fine film
on rice pudding flecked with nutmeg.

I ask to listen to her chest — she hesitates,
trembles her fingers over pearl buttons,
peels away the edge of a matted camisole,
seeped with the sweet musk of decay.

She shows me only the ulcerated edge,
concealed under a makeshift dressing.
I have never seen a tumour so advanced
and try not to let her read my face.

I ask gently why she had kept this hidden
for so long — her doctor visited every month.
She didn't want to upset such a lovely man,
she grasps my wrist, begs me not to tell him.

TIME TO HEAL

i.m. Dr Arthur Brock,
Wilfred Owen's doctor at Craiglockhart Hospital Edinburgh

Some nights their words seep through my dreams,
night terrors that drip with slaughter, men caught
on snarls of wire, noiseless dead in the thick darkness.

These men have become like the fragments of their minds.
I coax them to share what they have witnessed in daylight
to help them banish phantoms that stalk their sleep.

Owen often walks with Sassoon down the sloping lawns,
tells me he is the dark star in Sassoon's orbit.
There is a growing tenderness between them.

Our first meeting; the loose uniform, pallid skin
grey as smoked tallow-wax, the spring-loaded startle
at the rattle of a window, the tremor clattering his teacup.

Even his stammer settles when he reads out his poems
as if it were holding back horrors he could only express
on the page. Sassoon thinks he shows great promise.

I wake early thinking of my patients. Mist creeps over
the meadow, wraps slate rooftops. The Firth of Forth
shines a ribbon of light. As if nothing has changed.

ALBERT

He pulls his covers to his chin,
pegs them with rusted fingers,
his oxygen mask pushed up
like the cap he wore in the Hussars.

The Consultant, a voice smooth
as molasses, peers over half moons
to persuade Albert to take his tablets.
He cups his ear, scrinches his face.

In the night-hush of the ward
light spills from the nurses station.
Albert beckons me, says not to worry.
He is on his own now.

I like that he always calls me Maid
despite the new stiff white coat
carving crescents in my calves.
He worries it is past my bedtime.

While he sleeps I slide his mask down
to ease the rasps of breath.
I find his stash of tablets smuggled
in the shrug of his shoulders.

In the morning his bed is stripped
down to the shiny plastic cover,
his scant belongings parcelled up
for no one to collect.

ARTIST WITH A SCALPEL

after Bonjour Professor Calne, John Bellany

I turn his hands over in mine
his yellowed palms flushed pink
with toxins from his failing liver.
Oil paint has seeped into the creases,
stained cuticles etched in charcoal.
His abdomen is my canvas.

*

I press the tip of my scalpel blade,
make the first bold clean incision
watch beads of crimson ooze coalesce
in a line, a pout of fat opens beneath
as I cauterise through silvered fascia,

muscle fibres, pearlescent peritoneum
lifting it between the splayed web
of my gloved fingers, to protect organs
beneath, explore his abdominal cavity's
secrets with the crook of my fingers.

*

As soon as he comes round he needs
drawing paper to prove he is alive,
calls his pencils analgesics.
Now his paintings blaze with colour.

WATER THERAPY

She lowers him into the warm water,
    cushions his head on her shoulder,
cups his chin, murmurs close in,
    you will get better, you'll see.
His eyes squeezed shut, fists bunched,
    he can't look at his broken body.
They move in deep together,
    rocked on pleats of ripples.
Freed from the pull of gravity,
    buoyed up, his limbs loosen.
Once he's safe in her firm embrace
    she slowly releases her grip,
gently holds the pietà pale boy,
    draped across her arms,
until she knows he is ready
        to float free.

OBSESSION

Every morning she lurks
outside Surgery—waiting
—hoping to see him.

Trussed in her raincoat
in all weathers. On visits,
he had barely noticed her.

After her mother died
the letters keep coming.
then gifts, hand knitted scarves,

cakes left at reception.
At first he tells nobody,
at his age he feels foolish.

It is now an open secret.
He dreads the smirks,
worse still, moist-eyed pity

from his young colleague,
her head tipped to one side.
He delays telling the police,

part of him feels sorry for her.
On his way home he buys flowers
like in the early days, for a wife

eager for his return. He doesn't see
the woman hiding in the porch until
a glint of metal catches the light.

NEIGHBOURHOOD WATCH

His old work-suit jacket droops from the bony hanger
of his shoulders, a twist of tea-stained hankie peeps

from a frayed pocket. He stops every few yards
to catch his breath, unaware if a car idles behind.

A daisy chain of watchers mark his route
through raised curtains, chatter the airwaves.

In the Co-op he puzzles over the cold cabinet,
a tile of tissue, crimson flecked, stuck to his chin.

The wire basket snags on a dangling button, tangles
on the shopping bag his wife always used to carry,

neat zipped-up moc-croc. I hover, watch what he selects:
a frozen chicken pie for one, a small bottle of Guinness,

value choc-chip biscuits. He talks if we walk up the hill
together, on other days he says he can't stop.

He must hurry home to check on his wife
in case she left the gas on.

SPARROW

Her prom dress hangs
in the spare room,
A cage of stiff petticoats,
the bodice droops in folds
like ageing skin.

At each meal
the same tricks.
She pecks
at the insides
of sandwiches,
tucks morsels
under her fork.

Always a baggy jumper
thumbs poke through
frayed cuffs,
her face dusted
with down
soft as feathers.

Hollowed out,
she thinks her pain
is locked away.
Worried to startle her
we watch,
waiting for
her fall.

RUNNING

After it happened all I could do
was to listen to her replay every detail
to try and make sense of it.

The arum lilies, rain skittering
over fogged windows,
a heavy smell of spilled pollen,

her saying *Doctor, I can't do this.*

I still see her running
along the tow path, cap pulled down,
earphones in, staring ahead.

Trying to outrun grief
holding her son's ghost in her throat.
She never stops to talk.

SAVING ANDY WARHOL

i.m Giuseppe Rossi, Surgeon, Columbus Hospital, NYC

I'm about to peel off my scrubs,
humming along to *Mrs Robinson.*
I've promised to take my boy, Roberto,
to see the *New York Yankees* play
the *Minnesota Twins.* A call from ER,
another gunshot victim, white male,
undernourished, probably another
of our homeless from Union Square.
He's bleeding out, thready pulse.
They need me back in theatre
now. My intern is ready to certify him
clinically dead. Open heart massage
and 12 units later he's stable.
We trace the bullet from his right side
into his lung. It must have ricocheted
through his liver, gallbladder and spleen.
Closure is tricky, his abdomen a mess,
criss-crossed with incisions. His mother
keeps vigil, a stooped grey-haired babushka
in a threadbare coat, thick black stockings
with runs. She plucks at my sleeve
who would do this to my Andy?
I promise his wig will be on when he wakes.
I can hear my mother, *come home Giuseppe*
before they shoot you too. Afterwards
my patient tells me, *I am not afraid to die;*
I just don't want to be there when it happens.

23

SURVEILLANCE

She heard it again last night,
a rattle wrapped in the rain,
pebble-dashing the window.

A scrabble outside her door,
calling her name. Eyes peer
through the letter box.

Somebody moves her clothes,
tears her magazines. She keeps watch
at her window, nets drawn back.

A little girl, in a white nightdress,
comes after dark to sit with her
on the arm of her sofa.

That doctor again with the silk voice.
*Elsie it's me — I'm coming back
soon with someone who can help.*

The post box has a double,
upside down, shimmering in puddles.
Another slit to watch her through.

UNDERCOVER

Sat at the back of the waiting room
dressed in a beige, his windcheater
zipped up, he fades into the walls.

He brings War and Peace to remind
me to keep to time. I call his name
watch how he struggles to heave

his stiff frame from the chair.
Trapped inside his rigid body
like an insect entombed in amber.

I offer my arm, he shuffles small steps,
ask him if he's undercover. He reveals
he was once a commando in the jungle.

We both forget what he came for
and my surgery runs late again.

BOY

Most mornings, I glimpse the boy
walking to school. His shoes
trodden down at the back.

He trails behind, at the back
apart from the scuffle of boys,
I wonder if they laugh at his shoes.

He looks downtrodden, not just the shoes.
I wonder if his mother is back.
The egg shell pale boy.

I worry about the boy with the ill-fitting shoes alone at the back.

CARING FOR FRIDA

'Dr Eloesser, my doctor and my best friend'.

She has to sit to work now. Splashes of oil-paint catch
in the folds of fabric in her lap where the easel nestles.
Her speckled funerary beads streaked with brush strokes.

Each time our lives touch I see a different face of Frida.
To others she seems to have mastery over her suffering.
Swathed in shawls she conceals her crushed body

in billowing ground-skimming skirts, voluminous blouses
embellished with embroidery; lapis lazuli hummingbirds,
sunset-orange marigolds. Her gift to me, a self-portrait,

her hair braided with coral bougainvillaea, dark brows
meet like rooks' wings. A thorn necklace pierces her.

AFTER HOURS

A dusty electric fire, its purple-plaited lead
tied in a coil, unplugged on the hearth. I try
and persuade her to keep warm, show her

my blanched fingers, so cold they match hers.
I find a rug to tuck around her knees. Adjust
her trolley on wheels so she can still reach

her spectacles, the half-eaten packet of Rich Tea
and a thumbed copy of The Lady. In the night
I hear fire engines, smell the smouldering flex

the blanket fringe snagged in the rusty heater,
flapping blue-chequered police incident tape
cordoning off the road. Concerned neighbours

in dressing gowns, crowd around the ambulance.
I wake early, take a detour on my way to surgery.
Her bungalow is still intact in the sleeping cul-de-sac.

CRITICAL INCIDENT

someone somewhere is shouting
bradycardia bay 6
note the time
her trolley tipped head down
she's a girl doing a handstand
her hair hanging free
looking at the world upside down
she's cold   so cold
that word again
b-r-a-d-y-c-a-r-d-i-a
a slowed gramophone record
a gloved hand holds her arm
tap-tapping the crease of her elbow
she smells rubber on her face
the foreshore when the tide is out
a whistle of waves   more voices
heart rate still slow   note the time
bradycardia protocol   bolus
she tries to roll the word bolus
her mouth fills with marbles
bolus for bradycardia   so funny
nobody is laughing
the masks loom over her
their eyes upside down
ask if she is still cold
she feels the cold infusion
trickle ice through her hand
she is floating on a ripple of waves
hovering over her own reflection

*bradycardia - a slow heart rate

SAFE SPACE

He left his picture behind,
crumpled in a flimsy toybox,
scribbled with crimson crayon.

A winged woman with horns
holds a scythe, grinning.
A sharp stack of stickle bricks,

brittle plastic horses tangled
in a knot of string. Two floor fans
hang their heads scanning

the mud-brown floor
for his dropped secrets.
A smear of daylight sneaks

through frosted glass. The couch
with a black plastic protector
hides scuffs from small shoes.

The only splash of colour
an emerald green sign —
a boy running for the exit.

WATCHING VINCENT

After Dr Peyron, Van Gogh's doctor at the asylum in St Remy

On the first morning he set up his easel in the walled garden.
My other patients watch him work in silence or shuffle past.

He calls them his companions in misfortune. I begin
to notice my surroundings through an artist's eye, how

the wheat ripples sulphur-yellow, copper and bronze,
violet-blue olive trees sometimes silver, sometimes bluer,

the first emerald spring shoots splashed crimson with poppies.
He talks of the beautiful melancholy of the ravine,

finds sprigs of rosemary and thyme in the scorched grass
for his bedroom. He knows, when the mistral ribbons

through limestone rock a terrible terror and horror seize him,
prevent him thinking. Here in Provence we know it, call it

'the idiot wind'. He finds consolation at night looking out
beyond the bars of his window, to see Jupiter shimmer

for him, in a cobalt sky. He tells me the sight of stars always
makes him dream. He painted branches of our almond tree,

a scatter of petals against an azure canvas, to hang
above his nephew's crib. For his namesake, Vincent, he sung

a lullaby in colour. Vincent tells me how he longs
for autumn, chill October, the wistfulness of the year end.

BURNOUT

One winter Monday morning he left.
His gold pen nib bled a pool of ink
into the blotter. A letter half opened,
phone turned off, stethoscope coiled
in his jacket pocket. The back door, ajar
tapped time against the frame.

That night they found him walking, alone
along the banks of the Dart.

He never said why, on that day,
he could not soak up more sorrow.
In his studio, soothed by the hum
and whirr of his potter's wheel,
he cups and smooths soft clay.
It responds to his touch.

ACKNOWLEDGEMENTS

Albert first published in the NHS Anthology *These are the Hands*

First Do No Harm awarded first prize in the Hippocrates Prize 2020

Second Opinion awarded joint third prize in the Hippocrates Prize 2020

Undercover and *A Routine Housecall* commended in The Hippocrates Prize 2020

Obsession first appeared in *The Poetry Shed*

Water Therapy published in the *Alchemy Spoon Issue 4*

Peggy and George commended in the Hippocrates Prize 2019

Boy is on The Poetry School website

Safe Space published in *The Alchemy Spoon Issue 7*

Changeling commended in The Hippocrates Prize 2022

Time to Heal short listed in the Wells Poetry Competition 2021

Surveillance online in Ink Sweat & Tears 2023

Running shortlisted for the Brain Dempsey Memorial Prize 2023

Caring for Frida, Highly Commended & *Artist with a Scalpel* shortlisted for the Artemesia Arts Poetry Competition 2023

Thank you to my tutors at The Poetry School, Tamar Yoseloff, Glyn Maxwell and Jacqueline Saphra and to Rebecca Goss for her ongoing advice and support. Special thanks to my poetry friends Diana Cant, Vanessa Lampert, Roger Bloor, Mary Mulholland, Sara Levy, Alexandra Corrin-Tachibana, Erica Jane Morris, Simon Freeman and Sue Davies for their feedback and encouragement, the South Kensington stanza group and most of all to my husband Ted, my first reader, my lovely family and my dear friend John Sedgwick for sharing his love of poetry with m⟩ Many thanks to Mark Davidson at The Hedgehog Press for publishing my poems.